First Facts

Spotlight on the Continents

SPOTLIGHT ON
AFRICA

by A. R. Schaefer

CAPSTONE PRESS
a capstone imprint

First Facts is published by Capstone Press,
151 Good Counsel Drive, P.O. Box 669, Mankato, Minnesota 56002.
www.capstonepub.com

Books published by Capstone Press are manufactured with paper
containing at least 10 percent post-consumer waste.

Library of Congress Cataloging-in-Publication Data
Schaefer, A. R. (Adam Richard), 1976–
 Spotlight on Africa / by A. R. Schaefer.
   p. cm.—(First facts. Spotlight on the continents)
 Summary: "An introduction to Africa including climate, landforms, plants, animals,
and people"—Provided by publisher.
 Includes bibliographical references and index.
 ISBN 978-1-4296-6624-4 (library binding)
 1. Africa—Juvenile literature. I. Title.
 DT3.S326 2011
 960—dc22
                          2010037093

Editorial Credits
Lori Shores, editor; Gene Bentdahl, designer; Laura Manthe, production specialist

Photo Credits
Alamy/Jacques Jangoux, 12; Peter Anderson, 19; Wayne HUTCHINSON, 18
Corbis/Royalty Free, 9 (bottom right)
Corel, 13, 16
DigitalVision, 14 (top left)
Dreamstime.com/104paul, cover
Photodisc, 9 (bottom left)
Shutterstock/acequestions, 14 (top right); Arvind Balaraman, 20; David Peta, 1; POZZO
    DI BORGO Thomas, 9 (top); Steffen Foerster Photography, 14 (bottom)

Artistic Effects
Shutterstock/seed

Essential content terms are **bold** and are defined at the bottom of the page
where they first appear.

Printed in the United States of America in Melrose Park, Illinois.
092010   005935LKS11

TABLE OF CONTENTS

Africa 5

Fast Facts about Africa 6

Climate 8

Landforms 11

Plants 12

Animals 15

People 17

Living in Africa 18

Africa and the World 21

Glossary 22

Read More 23

Internet Sites 23

Index 24

CONTINENTS OF THE WORLD

AFRICA

Many scientists believe the world's second largest **continent** is the place where people first lived. Human bones found in Africa are millions of years old. Today people of different **cultures**, races, and religions call Africa home.

continent—one of Earth's seven large landmasses
culture—a people's way of life, ideas, customs, and traditions

FAST FACTS ABOUT
AFRICA

- **Population:** 1.03 billion

- **Number of countries:** 53

- **Largest cities:** Cairo, Egypt; Lagos, Nigeria; Kinshasa, Democratic Republic of the Congo

- **Longest river:** Nile, 4,160 miles (6,695 kilometers)

- **Highest point:** Kilimanjaro, 19,341 feet (5,895 meters)

- **Lowest point:** Lake Assal, 515 feet (157 meters) below sea level

COUNTRIES OF AFRICA

EUROPE

ASIA

MEDITERRANEAN
SEA

CANARY ISLANDS
(SPAIN)

MOROCCO

TUNISIA

LIBYA

EGYPT

RED SEA

WESTERN SAHARA

ALGERIA

CAPE VERDE

MAURITANIA

MALI

NIGER

CHAD

SUDAN

ERITREA

DJIBOUTI

SENEGAL

GAMBIA

GUINEA-BISSAU

GUINEA

BURKINA
FASO

BENIN

NIGERIA

CENTRAL AFRICAN
REPUBLIC

ETHIOPIA

SOMALIA

SIERRA LEONE

LIBERIA

IVORY COAST

GHANA

TOGO

CAMEROON

EQUATORIAL GUINEA

GABON

CONGO

UGANDA

RWANDA

KENYA

BURUNDI

SÃO TOMÉ & PRINCIPE

DEMOCRATIC REPUBLIC
OF THE CONGO

TANZANIA

SEYCHELLES

CABINDA
(ANGOLA)

ATLANTIC
OCEAN

ANGOLA

ZAMBIA

MALAWI

MOZAMBIQUE

COMOROS

MADAGASCAR

MAURITIUS

RÉUNION
(FRANCE)

ZIMBABWE

Kilometers
0   500   1000

N
W   E
S

NAMIBIA

BOTSWANA

0   620
Miles

SWAZILAND

INDIAN
OCEAN

SOUTH AFRICA

LESOTHO

CLIMATE

Deserts, rain forests, and **savannas** make up Africa. Deserts cover northern Africa and parts of the south. These areas sometimes don't get rain for months. Central Africa is mostly covered in hot, wet **rain forests**. Rain falls here nearly every day. Savannas cover most of the south. They are also found below the northern deserts. These hot grasslands get less rain.

savanna—a flat, grassy area of land with few trees
rain forest—a thick forest where a great deal of rain falls

LANDFORMS OF AFRICA

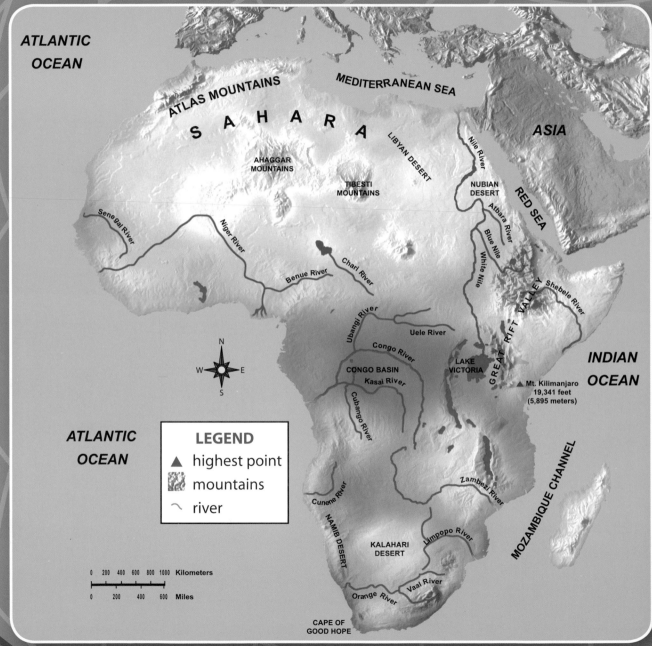

ATLANTIC OCEAN

MEDITERRANEAN SEA

ATLAS MOUNTAINS

S A H A R A

AHAGGAR MOUNTAINS

TIBESTI MOUNTAINS

LIBYAN DESERT

ASIA

NUBIAN DESERT

Nile River

Atbara River

Blue Nile

White Nile

RED SEA

Senegal River

Niger River

Benue River

Chari River

Ubangi River

Uele River

Congo River

CONGO BASIN

Kasai River

Cubango River

Shebele River

GREAT RIFT VALLEY

LAKE VICTORIA

INDIAN OCEAN

▲ Mt. Kilimanjaro
19,341 feet
(5,895 meters)

N
W   E
S

ATLANTIC OCEAN

LEGEND
▲ highest point
mountains
⌢ river

Zambezi River

MOZAMBIQUE CHANNEL

Cunene River

NAMIB DESERT

KALAHARI DESERT

Limpopo River

Orange River

Vaal River

CAPE OF GOOD HOPE

| 0 | 200 | 400 | 600 | 800 | 1000 | Kilometers |

| 0 | 200 | 400 | 600 | Miles |

LANDFORMS

Africa has some of the largest and longest landforms. The Sahara is one of the world's largest deserts. The Great Rift Valley is one of the largest cracks in the Earth's **crust**. Near this valley sits Lake Victoria, the second largest freshwater lake in the world. The Nile river drains from Lake Victoria. It is the world's longest river.

crust—the hard outer layer of Earth

PLANTS

Thousands of plants grow in Africa's rain forests. Some plants provide food for people. Other plants are used to make medicine.

Fewer plants grow in Africa's savannas and deserts. Savanna and desert plants may wait weeks for rain. Long roots help short bushes, grasses, and trees reach underground water.

ANIMALS

Millions of animals live in African rain forests. Parrots sing loudly while chimpanzees swing from trees. Gorillas eat fruit and leaves while snakes hunt small animals.

Africa's hot savannas are also home to many animals. Lions and cheetahs chase zebras. Elephants roll in the mud. Giraffes stretch their long necks to eat from treetops.

POPULATION DENSITY OF AFRICA

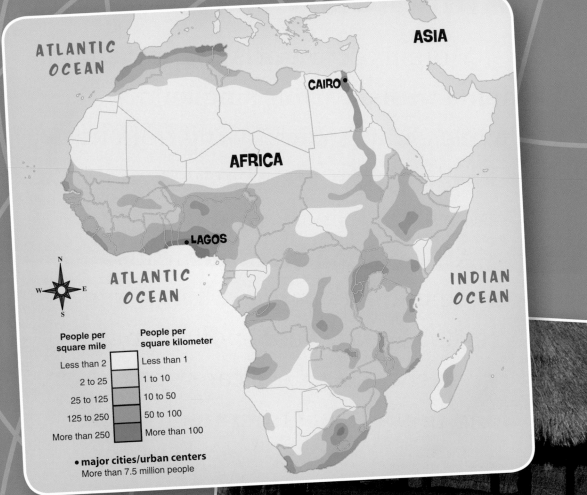

ATLANTIC OCEAN

ASIA

CAIRO

AFRICA

• LAGOS

ATLANTIC OCEAN

INDIAN OCEAN

N
W E
S

People per square mile

Less than 2
2 to 25
25 to 125
125 to 250
More than 250

People per square kilometer

Less than 1
1 to 10
10 to 50
50 to 100
More than 100

• **major cities/urban centers**
More than 7.5 million people

PEOPLE

More than half of Africa's people live in villages. But more people move to cities each year. They hope to find health care, cleaner water, and jobs.

Africa is the most **multilingual** continent in the world. More than 1,000 languages are spoken on the continent. Many Africans speak more than one language. Arabic, Swahili, and Hausa are the most common.

multilingual—using several languages

LIVING IN AFRICA

Africans' lives are shaped by the areas where they live. In the north, people eat flat breads and other foods made from grains. Rice and corn are more common in the south.

In modern cities, people have many housing choices. But in villages, most people live in homes made from dried mud or stone.

AFRICA AND THE WORLD

Africa is often called the birthplace of **humanity**. As Africans moved, their cultures spread across the world. Today, people around the world enjoy African music. Rock, pop, jazz, and other styles of music have roots in African music. Traditional African art and clothing have also reached beyond the edges of this continent.

humanity—all human beings

GLOSSARY

continent (KAHN-tuh-nuhnt)—one of Earth's seven large landmasses

crust (KRUHST)—the hard outer layer of the Earth

culture (KUHL-chuhr)—a people's way of life, ideas, customs, and traditions

humanity (hyoo-MAN-uh-tee)—all human beings

multilingual (muhl-tee-LING-wuhl)—able to speak several languages

rain forest (RAYN FOR-ist)—a thick forest where a great deal of rain falls

savanna (suh-VAN-uh)—a flat, grassy area of land with few trees

READ MORE

Friedman, Mel. *Africa*. A True Book. New York: Children's Press, 2009.

Tuchman, Gail. *Safari*. Washington, D.C.: National Geographic, 2010.

Underwood, Deborah. *Africa*. Exploring Continents. Chicago: Heinemann Library, 2007.

INTERNET SITES

FactHound offers a safe, fun way to find Internet sites related to this book. All of the sites on FactHound have been researched by our staff.

Here's all you do:

Visit *www.facthound.com*

Type in this code: 9781429666244

Super-cool stuff! Check out projects, games and lots more at **www.capstonekids.com**

INDEX

animals, 15
art, 21

cities, 6, 17, 19
climate, 8
clothing, 21
countries, 6
cultures, 5, 21

deserts, 8, 11, 13

food, 12, 18

Great Rift Valley, 11

highest point, 6
housing, 19

Kilimanjaro, 6

Lake Assal, 6
Lake Victoria, 11

languages, 17
longest river, 6, 11
lowest point, 6

music, 21

Nile, 6, 11

people, 5, 12, 17, 18, 19, 21
plants, 12–13
population, 6

rain, 8, 13
rain forests, 8, 12, 15
religions, 5

Sahara, 11
savannas, 8, 13, 15
size, 5

villages, 17, 19